THE PRAIRIE

CHARLES ROTTER

CREATIVE EDUCATION

Designed by Rita Marshall
with the help of Thomas Lawton

Published by Creative Education
123 South Broad Street,
Mankato, Minnesota 56001
Creative Education is an imprint
of Creative Education, Inc.

Photography by Peter Arnold, Inc.
(Tom Adams), Tom Bean, Gary
Braasch, Comstock (George Gerster),
F-Stock (Leland Howard), Photo
Researchers (Nick Bergkessel, Phil
Farnes, Francois Gohier, Rod
Planck), Tom Stack & Associates
(Larry Brock, Jeff Foott, Thomas
Kitchin, Gary Milburn, Brian
Parker, Rod Planck, John Shaw,
Diana L. Stratton, Chase Swift),
Larry Ulrich and Visuals Unlimited

Library of Congress
Cataloging-in-Publication Data

Rotter, Charles.
The prairie / written by Charles
Murray Rotter.
Summary: An introductory book on
grasslands, with emphasis on the
North American prairie, and
including information on vegetation,
animal life, human impact, and need
for preservation.
ISBN 0-88682-598-9
1. Prairies—North America—
Juvenile literature. 2. Prairie
ecology—North America—Juvenile
literature. 3. Prairie conservation
—North America—Juvenile
literature. [1. Grasslands.
2. Prairies.] I. Title. 92-44822
QH102.R67 1993 CIP
574.5' 2643' 097—dc20 AC

7

People often describe prairies or grass- lands by listing how they differ from other regions. For example, grasslands are flatter and drier than mountainous areas. They are less densely overgrown than jungles, and a bit more humid and hospitable than deserts. Describing what grasslands are not, rather than what they are, however, does them a great disservice.

Dawn at Badlands National Park, South Dakota.

8

Grasslands are living, vigorous regions, filled with many forms of life competing for survival. They are among the most fertile lands of our planet and play an important role in the global ecosystem. Agriculture in former grasslands accounts for about 70 percent of the food produced in the world. But grasslands are also fragile and easily destroyed. A greater understanding of them can help to slow or prevent the tragic loss of one of the world's great natural resources.

A wheat field in Saskatchewan, Canada.

Most grasslands are found in the middle of continents. They are far from the climate-moderating effect of oceans, so they are subject to wide daily and seasonal fluctuations of temperature and precipitation. Grasslands have annual precipitations of about 10 to 40 inches (25 to 102 cm). If they have less precipitation, they are likely to become deserts; more, and they are likely to become forests.

Flowers of the arctic tundra in Alaska.

Grasslands account for more than 30 percent of the earth's land area. The world's main grasslands are: the Eurasian steppe, which spans two continents all the way from Mongolia in Asia into eastern Europe; the African savannas; the llanos of Brazil; the pampas of Uruguay and Argentina; large tracts of frozen tundra throughout the arctic latitudes; and the North American prairie.

Tussocks (tuʃts) of grass in a wet meadow.

The first Europeans to encounter the North American prairie were Spanish conquistadors led by Francisco Vásquez de Coronado in 1541. They had been riding north in search of gold, and instead found an endless sea of grass. More than a century later, French explorers approached from the northeast. They named the grasslands they discovered with the French word for meadow: *Prairie*.

We still use the word prairie to describe the grasslands spanning the great plains of North America. The prairie forms a large triangle in the middle of the continent. Bordered by the Rocky Mountains on the west side, it stretches more than 2,000 miles (3,218 km) from the Northwest Territory of Canada to the U.S. state of Texas. The other two sides of the triangle connect in the Midwest and are each more than 1,000 miles (1,609 km) long. The prairie covers about 1.4 million square miles (3.6 million sq. km)—more than one-seventh of the total area of North America.

The grasslands of Nebraska.

Prairie grasses are divided into three general types, according to their heights: short-grasses, midgrasses, and tallgrasses. *Short-grasses*, which grow up to 18 inches (46 cm) high, prevail in the west, along the Rocky Mountains. Among the shortgrasses common to the prairie are grama grasses and buffalo grass. *Midgrasses*, which grow between 2 and 4 feet (61 and 122 cm) high, dominate in the geographic center of the prairie. Needlegrasses, little bluestem, and foxtail barley are examples of midgrasses. *Tallgrasses*, which usually grow over 5 feet (1.5 m) high and sometimes as high as 12 feet (3.7 m), are most common throughout the eastern prairie. Common tallgrass varieties are big bluestem, cordgrass, and Indian grass.

Tallgrasses of the Iowa prairie.

The reason these grasses grow where they do is simple: Shortgrasses need less rainfall than midgrasses, which in turn require less moisture than tallgrasses. The total annual rainfall of the prairie steadily increases from west to east. This steady increase in precipitation is due to the Rocky Mountains. As air from the West Coast rises over the mountains, it cools, and much of its moisture condenses as rain or snow on the upwind or *Windward* side. This creates a region of little rainfall—known as a rain shadow—on the downwind or *Leeward* side of the mountain. As the air heads east, it is supplied with moisture from other sources in the north and south, and the annual rainfall increases.

The pampas of Argentina.

19

Because the eastern prairie gets more precipitation than the west, it supports a wider
variety of plants and animals. Hundreds of
different grasses can exist within a single
acre. The soils are rich black topsoils called
Mollisols. The mollisols of the eastern prairie are among the most fertile and productive
in the world. A great deal of North American
agriculture, particularly corn, wheat, and
soybean production, has developed in lands
of the eastern prairie.

The rich soil of the eastern prairie.

Grasses are ideally suited for life on the prairie. They can survive conditions such as drought, freezing temperatures, drying winds, and grazing animals—conditions that would kill many other plants. The grass grows thick and dense, forming a tough layer of matted soil called *Sod.* A thick layer of sod can keep the roots from freezing in the winter and even insulate the underground part of the plant from the heat of a brushfire. Prairie grasses also have deep and efficient root systems that can seek out moisture located far underground. And because the grass grows from the base of a blade, it continues to grow if the blade is cut.

Along with the many different types of grasses growing on the prairie, hundreds of

broad-leaved herbs called *Forbs* inhabit the prairie. Typical prairie forbs are fleabane, milkweed, and gentian. Many of these herbs were used as medicines by both Native Americans and European settlers. For example, the Omaha Indians used milkweed roots to make a salve for wounds. The European settlers used the same roots to treat respiratory ailments.

Together, the grasses and forbs form the heart of the *Prairie Ecosystem*. They are the base of the food chain upon which all other forms of prairie life depend. The plants of the prairie, along with all the animals inhabiting it, form a complex and interdependent web of life competing for survival.

Page 20: Deep root systems enable prairie grasses to survive.
Page 21: A milkweed pod.

Before Europeans imported horses, cattle, and sheep, only two large grass-eating animals roamed the prairie—the mighty bison and the swift pronghorn. While these two large mammals eat tremendous amounts of grass, they actually help to maintain a healthy supply of grass as well. By clearing away old growth while feeding and by breaking up the sod with their sharp hooves, these animals inadvertently till the soil, promoting the growth of new and healthy plants. The large herbivores also trample young trees at the prairie margin, keeping them from invading the grasslands. And, of course, the animals' droppings are a source of nutrients for the growing plants.

Cordgrass, common in the eastern prairie.

24

Native Americans hunted for centuries without depleting the *Bison,* which numbered in the tens of millions. European hunters in the nineteenth century, however, made short work of the animals. Modern rifles enabled these hunters to kill hundreds of bison at a time. Native Americans hunted only out of need, but the new arrivals hunted for sport and profit, slaughtering the herds in staggering numbers. In a matter of decades, bison were hunted almost to extinction. A small number of them—only about 500—escaped the hunters. Now kept in refuges and on ranches, their numbers have increased into the tens of thousands. But the bison will never again darken the prairies from horizon to horizon.

Bison grazing in Yellowstone National Park.

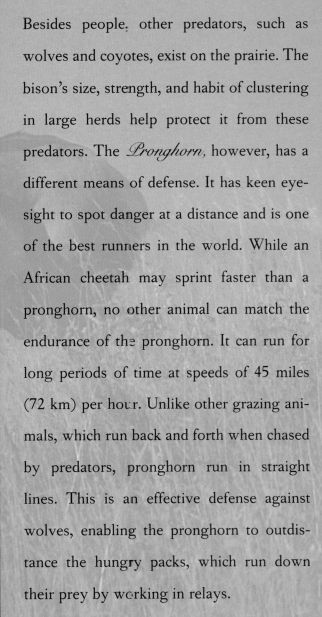

Besides people, other predators, such as wolves and coyotes, exist on the prairie. The bison's size, strength, and habit of clustering in large herds help protect it from these predators. The *Pronghorn,* however, has a different means of defense. It has keen eyesight to spot danger at a distance and is one of the best runners in the world. While an African cheetah may sprint faster than a pronghorn, no other animal can match the endurance of the pronghorn. It can run for long periods of time at speeds of 45 miles (72 km) per hour. Unlike other grazing animals, which run back and forth when chased by predators, pronghorn run in straight lines. This is an effective defense against wolves, enabling the pronghorn to outdistance the hungry packs, which run down their prey by working in relays.

A pronghorn buck with three does.

28

In addition to pronghorn and bison, many rodents live off the prairie grasses. These small burrowing mammals are often social and may live in large cooperative communities. The *Prairie Dog* is the most social of the rodents. It lives in clans called *Coteries*. The coteries sometimes include more than a dozen prairie dogs who feed, play, and groom together.

Young prairie dogs.

Members of a coterie are usually very protective of their territory, but in times of danger, they allow other prairie dogs to use their burrows to hide from predators such as hawks or coyotes. Sometimes the coteries even live side by side, forming the prairie dog equivalent of small towns—or even cities. At the turn of the century, a community of prairie dogs in Texas reportedly covered 25,000 acres (10,125 hectares) and contained 400 million prairie dogs.

30

The birds of the prairie are also uniquely qualified to survive in the grasslands. Most of them need less water, eat more seeds, and fly together in groups more often than birds in other climates. Some of them, such as the *Prairie Chicken,* are ground dwellers, spending most of their time roaming on foot in search of food.

A male prairie chicken in a mating display.
Inset: A nematode feeds on algae.

31

While mammals and birds may be the most noticeable animal life on the prairie, they are far outnumbered by smaller animals that are much harder to see. Most of the creatures that inhabit the prairie live deep within the grass and the soil. Insects and unsegmented worms called *Nematodes* consume far more grass and plants than all the mammals and birds put together. Insects, worms, nematodes, fungi, microscopic bacteria, and protozoans are all part of the soil ecosystem. Some benefit the grasses; others do not. But almost all of them play some crucial role in stabilizing the interdependent community.

Occasionally, however, the prairie may seem anything but stable. For example, *Locusts,* a type of grasshopper, sometimes multiply out of control. When this happens, billions of locusts cover the sky like clouds, flying in search of food. They strip all vegetation in their path, destroying crops and leaving only barren fields behind them. Eventually, the swarm dies out due to a lack of food, a change in climate, or an increase in its natural enemies, such as birds. Fortunately, because the prairie grasses have such large underground root systems, they can grow back and replenish the plains even after the worst locust attack.

The Wyoming prairie.
Inset: A locust.

In this situation and others, the checks and balances of nature ensure that the ecosystem will not be permanently damaged by changing conditions. When people use the grasslands, however, these checks and balances often disappear. Unfortunately, grasslands that have been converted to agriculture may no longer be as resilient as they once were. Without the protective cover of sod, winds can carry off tons of precious *Topsoil*, robbing the land of its productivity.

A mustard field in bloom.

This is what happened in the United States during the *Dust Bowl* in the 1930s. Prolonged drought killed the crops, and because the sod had been plowed away, the dry winds stripped the topsoil off the farmland, filling the skies with clouds of dust. It was among the worst agricultural and environmental disasters in U.S. history. Some of the dust drifts piled up to 25 feet (7.6 m) high. In several states, the amount of dust blown into the atmosphere was enough to make people seriously ill.

Soil conservation methods, including terracing, windbreaks, and controlled grazing, can help protect the grasslands. But these practices are often expensive and may reduce farming profits. This pressures the world's farmers, who are often struggling financially, to put off using conservation measures. Eventually, new grassland is cleared to replace the ruined cropland, and the destructive cycle continues.

A dry, plowed field is stripped by the wind.

On the African continent, the main problem is *Overgrazing*. When domesticated animals are allowed to graze too long in one area, the root systems of the plants become damaged, and the soil erodes easily in dry weather. Overgrazing may even be partially responsible for the southerly advance of the Sahara Desert over the past 5,000 years. While climate changes are primarily responsible for this loss of more than 250,000 square miles (647,500 sq. km) of productive land, it is hard to say how much this process may have been accelerated by misuse. As the land becomes barren and people move on, all that is left is an unproductive desert landscape that may take centuries to recover—if it recovers at all. This process is known as *Desertification*.

Page 38: Overgrazing can have long-term consequences.
Page 39: The Sahara.

40

As world population and hunger increase geometrically, so does the pressure on *Grasslands* throughout the world. The people who can least afford to let the land rest and recover are the ones who will suffer later if conservation is not practiced. It is up to the entire world to understand, appreciate, and protect the fragile and productive environment of the world's grasslands.

A lightning storm over the plains of southeast Colorado.